Detective In
The Landscape
In South-East England

Detective In The Landscape
In South-East England

Marcus Crouch

With Photographs by the Author

Longman Young Books

LONGMAN GROUP LIMITED LONDON
Associated companies, branches and representatives throughout the world

First published 1972

ISBN 0 582 15070 1

*Set in 12/14 pt. Monotype Plantin, printed by photolithography,
and bound in Great Britain at The Pitman Press, Bath*

Contents

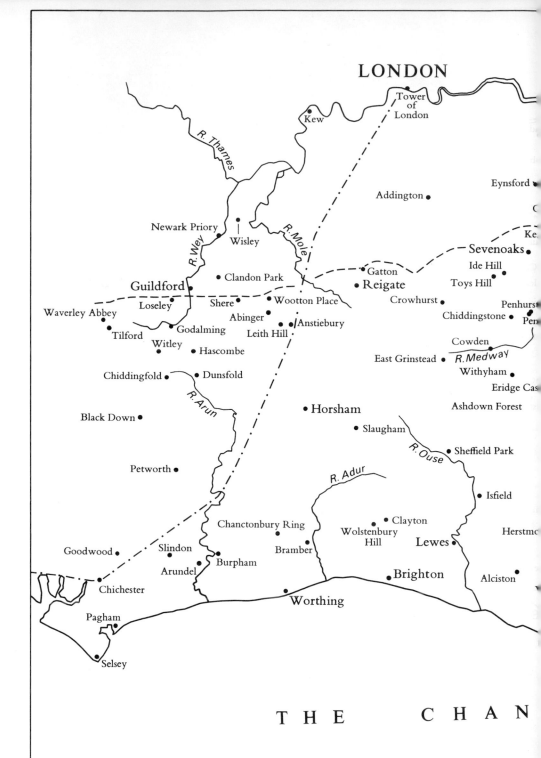

R. Thames

Cooling Castle

Upnor

Rochester

St. Nicholas-at-Wade

Reculver

Margate

Herne Bay

Birchington

R. Wantsum

St. Peter's-in-Thanet

Snodland

Kit's Coty

Sarre

Minster

Pegwell

Wrotham

Richborough

Bay

Aylesford

Harbledown

Canterbury

Maidstone

Shepway

Hollingbourne

Sandwich

Chilham

Leeds

Deal

Castle

stead

Yalding

Chart Sutton

idge

Wells

Ashford

Dover

Bayham

Biddenden

Mersham-le-Hatch

Cranbrook

Lympne

Folkestone

Tenterden

Hythe

R. Rother

Appledore

Newchurch

Oxney

Romney Marsh

Dymchurch

Old Romney

Burwash

Bodiam

New Romney

Rye

Lydd

Denge

Winchelsea

Dungeness

Forge

Battle

Pett

Hastings

**South-East
England**

evensey

Eastbourne

L

- - - - Pilgrims Way

- . - . - Stane Street

0   10   20 miles

FOR
OLIVE

Hops

1 The Civilest Part

Julius Caesar, speaking it is true from hearsay, called Kent the civilest part of Britain. As a Roman he did not think highly of barbarians in any country, but he saw that some of the savages across the Channel were readier than the rest for the blessings of the Roman peace.

When the barbarians nearly wrecked his plans so that he returned to the Continent with only a shadow of a victory, he may have been tempted to revise his opinion of them. Those who have

Chiddingfold, a village of the Surrey Weald

lived in the south-eastern counties during most of the centuries of history have never had any doubt about the accuracy of Caesar's words. The counties of Kent, Sussex and Surrey have been in the mainstream of English history for four thousand years and more. Invaders, missionaries, scholars, statesmen have all come into England through the Channel ports. Their main idea may have been to get to London as quickly as possible, but some of their wisdom and learning and strength brushed off on to the inhabitants of the south-eastern peninsula as they went.

No part of England has changed more greatly or more often. The very shape of the map has altered in the last two thousand years, as acres have been won from the sea and others lost to it. In the central area the pace of change was held back by a wide belt of dense forest. Progress and development made their way on either side of the forest, from the sea and the river. When the Wealden forest was at last destroyed, communication across the region became possible, and the face of the land underwent yet another change. Now it is changing again. The new invaders come not from overseas but from other parts of Britain where declining prosperity drives people to try their luck in the developing south. Other influences may soon make their mark on these three counties. Britain is looking towards Europe more than it has done since the Middle Ages. European unity, the Channel Tunnel, air and hover-craft routes, all make the Channel seem narrower and bring Europe closer to Kent and Sussex.

With such great and continuous changes and such a flow of new residents one might expect that the south-east would lack a regional character. It has not the clearly defined quality of detached and

self-contained regions like Wales and the Lake District. It does not cling to local characteristics as Lancashire and Yorkshire do. The elegant accents of the BBC and the rougher tones of Cockney have almost killed dialect; a few people, especially in the Weald, retain the old slow lilt and use a few ancient, colourful words, but they become fewer every year. The new invaders, however, are absorbed very quickly into the region, just as the Jutes and the Saxons, the Normans and the Flemings were. The population has always been mixed, and Yorkshiremen and Scots, however much they cling to their accents and yearn for their homeland hills, learn quickly to associate themselves with their new region.

Many of the new south-easterners come from districts which shared in the Industrial Revolution of the nineteenth century. Some of them are taking part in a similar revolution of the twentieth, working in new power, oil and transport enterprises which are transforming the region. More often the new residents are resident only; by day they join the mass migration to London, returning to the country or to provincial towns or more often to shapeless 'commuter' estates to sleep.

With all the pressures of modern industry and urban development the south-east has sometimes been in danger of disappearing for ever under a load of concrete and brick. Miraculously the countryside survives. Every day more lorries and cars hurtle along the trunk roads and the motorways. A network of minor roads is comparatively little used, and thousands of miles of bridleways and footpaths await the horseman and the walker.

Much of the history of England has been played out in the south-east. Every town, almost every village, has had a share in national events. The memories of great events and of great men are everywhere. It would be easy for the region to live on its memories. It continues to create new traditions, new myths.

I have not tried to squeeze into these few pages the events of four thousand years or to draw a complete picture of the crowded, prosperous region of today. Instead I have limited myself to picking up a handful of threads from the past and, where possible, following them through to the present. These are samples. Those who live in the region, or who visit it on holiday, may make them the starting-point for independent explorations and personal discoveries. There is plenty of material in the three counties for a lifetime of journeys, each full of expected and unexpected delights. Happily, this over-crowded corner of Britain still has pockets of quiet and neglected country, and places which are renowned for their place in history or as the home of makers of history are often rich in natural beauty.

Cement works in the Adur valley, Sussex

2 A Chalk Bowl

The key to the south country is chalk. Beyond the first men who with crude stone tools and weapons began their long journey towards civilization lay millions of years of change. The foundations were laid down layer by layer beneath the sea, then violent forces pushed and folded the strata of rock, raising and lowering them to produce in time the rough ground-plan of this country. What at last emerged was a high dome rising to its centre roughly halfway between the Channel and a northern river which became the Thames. The sandstone hump was scarred with the channels

15

of many rivers, flowing north and south from the watershed to find the sea. The sandstone formed a crust over the chalk foundations of the region. After many centuries of earth movement, heat, cold and torrents of rain, the crust cracked, broke up and was washed away leaving only the stumps of hills across the centre of the area. Instead of a dome—or an upturned bowl—a rimmed bowl began to appear, its edge of chalk and its middle an untidy hump of sandstone. Still the rivers flowed along their ancient courses, although now they seemed, contrary to nature, to find the hardest way to the sea through gaps in the chalk.

From these upheavals the landscape of the south-east at last emerged. It is an unusually symmetrical landscape. Two lines of chalk Down face one another, their steep escarpments looking inwards and undulating slopes facing outwards. Below the steep

Downs are two fertile valleys. Then come two parallel ridges, the northern more clearly defined and continuous than the southern. The rolling hills which are all that remains of the sandstone dome have on either side flat river valleys. The region has on its outer edge plains of very flat, newly formed land. So precisely is each half of the scene reproduced that it almost seems as if one is the mirror image of the other.

The Downs give the south-east its most familiar aspect. The North and South Downs run almost parallel courses until on their western borders they merge into the wide rolling tableland of the Hampshire heights. When men first came to live here the downs were heavily wooded. Changes in climate led to the drying out of the chalk; trees thinned out naturally and could more easily be

Chanctonbury Ring, Sussex

cleared by primitive farmers who ploughed the thin soil of the chalk terraces. The South Downs are still largely bare, except where modern foresters have planted conifers which tolerate these dry conditions; the North Downs are often clothed in woods, tall smooth beeches or dark evergreen box and yew. Only in the extreme east, where they roll towards the narrow seas, the North Downs raise bare crests to the sky. Where they reach the sea they form the famous white cliffs, falling sheer to pebbly beaches and continually crumbling away.

Originally the Downs were cultivated by Stone-Age farmers whose light ploughs could not break the heavy soil of the valleys. Then, for many centuries the hills became pasture, feeding the rich chalk grass to downland sheep. Pasture they stayed until the need to grow food in wartime forced twentieth-century farmers to plough the hill-tops again. Now, with mechanized ploughing, all

South Downs at Alciston,
Sussex

Sussex Weald,
Ashdown Forest

but the steepest slopes of the escarpment have gone under plough, and the rolling country between ridge and sea is given over to wheat and barley. In Surrey, behind the ridge of the Downs there are curious pockets of sandy country which produce the wide commons for which the county is famous. In agricultural terms they are unproductive and many acres are given over to golf courses and to the enjoyment of walking and riding.

In early times the downland ridges, and the sheltered terraces below their crests, were favoured highways. Trackways made by primitive travellers still remain on North and South Downs, sometimes as modern metalled highways, but more often as bridleways used only by horsemen and hikers.

Almost as distinctive as the long sweep of the Downs is the parallel ridge of the lower greensand which runs almost unbroken

The Weald of Kent, near Chiddingstone

from the Hampshire border to the sea near Folkestone. The green-sand hills are usually lower than the Downs but not much less steep. In the east the country is fully cultivated, but farther west there is some forestry and then much common land, including tracts of open heath and woodland like Ide Hill and Toys Hill in Kent and Leith Hill in Surrey which are owned on behalf of the public by the National Trust. The prospect from Leith Hill, where a brick tower enables the visitor to stand, for the only time in the south-east, a thousand feet above sea level, is the widest in the region, taking in the full range of the South Downs and the Weald and perhaps—although I have never seen it—the sea.

The wide tract below Leith Hill is part of the Weald. 'Weald' means 'forest' and the land between the greensand and the South Downs was for many centuries completely clothed with dense woodland. Much of the history of the Weald is explained by this fact, for the forest made a barrier across the middle of the region until well into the Middle Ages. There were few roads through it, and for a long time the only settlements were clearings where swineherds ran their pigs or a little primitive mining went on. We shall see later how the Weald was cleared and the landscape trans-formed, to produce the present fertile and beautiful area.

The sandy hills of the Weald are for the most part lower than the Downs, but in the west they rise at Black Down to a point not far below a thousand feet. The Wealden plain in Kent is the heart of the hop industry and there are many orchards, principally of apples. The land grows houses as well, many estates for London commuters and also some of the great palaces of seventeenth and eighteenth century gentlemen with vast parks around them.

On the lower flanks of both North and South Downs lies an area of very flat country bordering the Thames in the north and in the south lying along the coastal strip. These are the oldest popu-lated areas of the region. When most of central Sussex was given over to wild animals and a few wild men the coastal plain was highly populous and the peninsula of Selsey was a major centre of

Reed Beds in the Cuckmere Valley, Sussex

civilization which, in early Christian times, had its own cathedral. Farther east progress was held up by the presence of wide-spreading marshes and wide river estuaries. Gradually these acres were reclaimed and became good pasture and later rich arable land.

Except for the sandy commons of Surrey and west Kent there is very little waste in all this land. Good cornland, better fruit and hop country, some profitable market gardening, the pastures of Romney Marsh and Southdown sheep make this an important farming district. Every year an increased acreage goes over to housing, and land disappears under tarmac and concrete. Industry is on the increase, not only traditional industries like concrete and paper but new ones, all of which take their toll of the land. Surprisingly there is still much open country. In the Surrey hills I have walked for an hour without seeing a person or a house. There are miles of narrow roads through the Downs in Kent where one rarely sees a car. In parts of the South Downs the only company is that of sheep and skylarks. The chalk country of Kent and Sussex is famous for wild flowers and provides a home for some of the rarest and loveliest of English orchids. And for those who like fine scenery, the soft hills and the valleys of slow ambling streams offer pleasure and satisfaction quite different from, and not less deep, than that of wild mountain country.

The Long Man of Wilmington, Sussex

Iron Age camp on Wolstonbury Hill, Sussex

3 Invasion Coast

The Narrow Seas are so narrow that the cliffs of France can be seen from many points between Dover and Rye. The short voyage has always been favoured by migrants and invaders, and the tracks and roads leading from the Channel ports have seen most of the tribes and armies which came to Britain to burn, destroy and finally to settle. Stone and Bronze Age farmers, Iron Age warriors, Romans, Saxons, Danes, Normans, French, Flemings and Dutch—they all came this way and left their mark on the south-east.

The Strand Gate of Winchelsea, Sussex

Richborough, Kent: third-century walls

Some invaders came in peace, looking for land or work; most came for conquest and loot. What drove them was shortage of land. The sons—especially the younger sons—of European chiefs could find no place of their own and had to look westwards for a home. Often enough they had to fight for it against earlier settlers. Each wave of invaders was more violent than the last until towards the end of the pre-Christian era the south country was a battleground of tribes perpetually at war.

To this time the first great monuments, the hill-forts, belong. Iron Age tribes were expert in making large earthen camps, placed on a spur of the Downs or the greensand or on a coastal promontory. The earliest of the hill-forts consisted of a single bank and ditch protecting an oval or circular area of fairly flat ground. As enemies became more numerous and weapons more sophisticated, the design of the forts improved until they had multiple ramparts and guarded entrances. Many of them—now in open country—were surrounded by thick woodland. An enemy coming in force up to their steep banks would have to fight his way through a forest of spiked stakes and a high wooden fence.

When Julius Caesar attempted the conquest of Britain, he stormed one of these forts at Bigbury on the North Downs. Although he won victories he could not complete his conquest, and this was left to Roman armies almost ninety years later. The Roman conquest was based on a beachhead established in the mouth of the Wantsum, a sea-channel between Kent and Thanet. In a good defensive position here the Romans built a fortress, of earthworks and masonry, which became their main military depot during the four centuries of their stay in Britain. Much remains of the fortress of Richborough, some of it dating from the original Claudian invasion. A little later the Romans built a huge tower within the fort, perhaps a beacon tower and also a memorial to the conquest of Britain. The vast block on which this stood can still be seen. So can the walls of a later fort set up to discourage raiders along the coast. At a time of political unrest and bold piracy in the third century a ring of forts was slung along the coast; of these

Pegwell Bay, Kent: dragon-ship Hugin, a memorial to the Saxon invasions

Richborough was probably the most important and there were others at Reculver—guarding the northern mouth of the Wantsum, at Dover, Lympne and Pevensey.

The warlike Saxons who overran the country after the departure of the Romans were not great makers of fortresses. They were at first deeply suspicious of Roman buildings, which they left to fall into ruin; even when they got over their awe at the achievements of the past they still kept to their own ways. Sometimes they, and the Danes who later disputed the country with them, made earthen ramparts round a settlement to give it extra security, but these have usually disappeared under later work. The boundaries of a Saxon burgh remain at Coldred, near Dover, and a curious earth table in the Arun valley at Burpham may be of the same kind.

Normans who settled in England before the Conquest made themselves strongholds of earth and wooden stakes, and King Harold threw up a fortified mound on the heights above Dover. We shall be looking at Norman castles in another chapter.

We are accustomed to think of William the Conqueror's invasion as the last in our history, but the coast continued under attack. In the French wars English expeditionary forces won brilliant victories at Crecy and Agincourt, but citizens of the Channel ports and coastal villages lived in constant fear of seaborne raids by the French. The Cinque Ports—five ancient ports, Sandwich, Dover, Hythe, Romney, Hastings, along the coast, together with the twin towns of Rye and Winchelsea and many minor ports—were given privileges in return for supplying ships to fight the king's enemies. They paid for this by becoming the target for attacks across the Channel. Rye and Winchelsea suffered particularly badly and still show some of the scars.

To ward off these attacks new castles were built at weak points along the coast. Today Bodiam, in Sussex, may not seem near the sea, but the narrow Rother once spread wide between the hills and in favourable conditions French ships might sail as far inland as this. In face of this danger a knight who had fought the French on

Canterbury, West Gate: built in 1378

DEFENSIVE WORKS

Cooling Castle, Kent, 1381

Herstmonceux Castle, Sussex, a brick castle built in 1440

*Pages 30–31: Bodiam
Castle, Sussex, 1385*

*Royal Military Canal,
near Appledore*

their home ground got permission to build a fortress to defend Sussex 'against the king's enemies'. By a freak of chance Bodiam Castle remains perfect—or at least a perfect roofless shell. What the visitor may notice are the four drum towers at the corners, now beautifully reflected in the moat, but equally interesting is the great gatehouse, approached across the moat by a right-angled causeway designed to make direct assault almost impossible. Once on the causeway an attacker would still have to capture an island tower (now ruinous) while exposed to fire from the castle walls.

At Cooling, in the marshes of the Thames estuary, Lord Cobham built a formidable castle with a huge top-heavy gatehouse. This was designed 'in help of the cuntre', as a metal plaque on the tower proclaims. A third castle was at Saltwood, behind the Cinque Port of Hythe, where an old manor of the Archbishops of Canterbury was fortified and a very tall gatehouse built. All these castles have features in common with one another and with the great West Gate of Canterbury, and they may have shared the same architect, Henry Yevele.

The Hundred Years War came to an end, followed by years of civil war and then the Tudor peace. When Henry VIII broke with Rome the country was again threatened with invasion. Some of the spoils of the monasteries had to be spent on more coastal forts, this time designed to resist cannon-fire. Several of these so-called castles remain, the best of them at Deal. The threatened attack never came, but the castles were repaired and others added when the Invincible Armada was assembled in Spanish ports during the reign of Elizabeth. One of the new forts was at Upnor, guarding the mouth of the Medway. Eighty years later Upnor Castle played an inglorious part when the Dutch sailed past its guns and destroyed the English fleet at its moorings.

The next threat to the south coast came in the war with Napoleon. French troops massed at Boulogne, waiting for their fleet to gain temporary control of the Channel. The old forts were manned and new ones—squat drums called Martello towers—added. One weak point in the defences was the flat area of Romney Marsh. A deep canal was dug around the Marsh along the line of the old sea-coast. This Royal Military Canal was made in short straight sections, each angled to give advantage of fire to the defender. Nelson broke the French fleet at Trafalgar and the invasion never came. The Royal Military Canal remains to remind of a great peril.

Of the greater peril of Hitler's war there are innumerable relics in the south-east: block-houses by rivers, tank traps on remote beaches, wide fields marking the sites of Battle of Britain airfields, ruins resulting from enemy bombing, and in woodland weed-grown army camps, all evidence of the last occasion when the Channel served 'as a moat against the envy of less happier lands'.

The ruined harbour at Pagham, Sussex

4 Change and Decay

If one could see a two-thousand-year-old map of England to compare with one of the present day, the south-east would show greater changes than any other part of the country. It is not just that wide areas of deserted country have turned into dense cities. The profile of the country—its coastline—has been transformed.

Changes in coastline are usually a matter of profit and loss. The tides nibble away year after year at certain parts of the coast and push the resulting shingle until it builds up a new beach across the

Bed of the Wantsum, Minster, Kent

The Wantsum, Thanet: medieval embankment beside the channel

bay. Dungeness, the spit of land near the Kent-Sussex boundary, grows every year at the expense of the beaches towards Pett. The western promontory of Selsey Bill has been wearing away for many centuries, and the old capital of the South Saxons, cathedral and all, has been lost in the sea. A great harbour on the Selsey peninsula at Pagham has been blocked by the movement of the beach and turned into a shallow lagoon accessible only by small craft and seabirds.

There is scope for exploration in the lost seabed of the Wantsum. When Claudius Caesar's legions landed at Richborough the Wantsum was a deep channel between a half-mile and two miles wide which separated Thanet from the mainland of Kent. So it remained until well into the Middle Ages. The normal route from the English Channel to London port was along the Wantsum, cutting out the long passage around the North Foreland. The Wantsum was used by merchant ships and by Saxon and Danish raiders. Eventually the action of the tides combined with silt brought down by the River Stour to block the outlet at Sandwich and the Wantsum faded out of history. Natural forces and the work of landowners, including the monks of Minster Abbey, filled in its bed until now the Wantsum is barely to be distinguished from

Romney Marsh: the lost estuary of the Limen. On the cliffs to the left are fragments of the Roman fort of Portus Lemanis

Lympne Castle on the cliffs above Romney Marsh

CHANGING KENT

The decayed port of Old Romney

other drainage dykes which intersect the flat land between Reculver and Birchington.

Some clues for explorers of the bed of this lost sea are the villages of Sarre, which has lost its church and most of its houses, and St. Nicholas-at-Wade—the Wade was a low-tide ford across the channel to Thanet—the ruins at Reculver and Richborough, and the embankment called the Monks Wall which follows the eastern bank of the Wantsum within sight of the ancient settlement of Minster.

Romney Marsh—to be strictly correct one should say the Marshes of Romney, Walland and Denge—was made in part by natural forces, by the fall and rise of the land and by river silt and tide. Man's contribution to the process has been enormous. Perhaps, as the tradition goes, the Romans took a hand in it by making the two 'walls', Dymchurch and Rhee, which acted as breakwaters and helped to build up sand and silt into land. The work went on intermittently for centuries—and in a real sense still goes on, because the Marsh remains dry through pumping and sea-defence work.

One important actor in the drama of Romney Marsh is the River Rother. Today the Rother is an unimpressive stream which seems miscast for a major role, but it has been a maker and a destroyer. In Roman Britain the Rother flowed along the base of the greensand cliffs below Lympne to reach the sea where Hythe now stands. For much of this course it was a marshy estuary but with a good navigable channel up to the Roman Portus Lemanis and to Appledore and beyond. At some time in the Dark Ages the reclamation of the land and the action of tides caused the Rother to shift its course so that it reached the sea at Romney in a wide estuary with the ports of Old and New Romney on its shores and Lydd at the mouth. Then, in a great storm in 1287, the mouth of the river was blocked, and the Rother migrated again, to find the sea below the conical rock of Rye. In that same storm the port of Winchelsea was lost to the sea and King Edward I rebuilt it in a safe—unfortunately an unseaworthy—position on top of the cliffs.

The Shepway Cross, Lympne, Kent

Visiting the Marsh today, it is not too difficult to see evidence of growth and change. Between Old and New Romney the main road falls just short of the Rhee Wall and you may see the embankment as a slight rise in the fields parallel with the road. Each of the early settlements stands on a tiny hump lifting it above the level of the Marsh. (This is especially clear at Old Romney and Newchurch.) In a wet winter flood water turns Oxney into the Isle of Oxen again and you may see the old navigable channel flowing down from the Small Hythe—the haven of Tenterden. Best of all, standing by the Shepway Cross at Lympne—the Shepway was the Sheep-Way, a good name for the marshland pasture—you may see all the Marsh at one glance with its cliffs, its river-courses and its ports and settlements.

No other changes have been as spectacular as the transformation of Thanet and the Marsh. People moving from old homes to new have changed the countryside in its detail, producing in recent years the sprawling suburban estates on the London fringe and along each main railway line. The opposite process has also worked. When, in the fourteenth century, the terrible plague of the Black Death struck the country some villages were wiped out and were never resettled. This may have been the fate of Dode, in the North Downs not far from Gravesend. There was a little flint church here in Norman times and no doubt there was a village to go with it. Late in the nineteenth century a Mayor of Gravesend put in hand the restoration of the church, by then roofless, but the village had vanished and no sign remained that anyone had lived there since the Middle Ages.

The Black Death forced many farmers to change over from arable farming to sheep, which needed fewer men to do the work. Sheep farming became profitable and went on even when the population had made up its losses. There was no longer enough work in the villages to support the inhabitants. In areas where sheep were farmed on a larger scale, like Romney Marsh, villages

Hope All Saints, Romney Marsh

LOST VILLAGES

Dode, in the North Downs, Kent

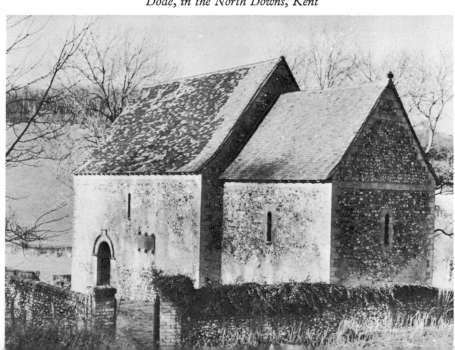

were abandoned. The houses, wooden-framed and wattle-walled, fell down and disappeared without trace. The churches lasted longer, being made of stone, but these too lost their roofs and the walls followed. On the Marsh there are six old parishes of which at best a few fragments of the church remain. The shifting of river courses brought ruin too to places like West Hythe which lost their trade when the old sea-water channels finally silted up.

Ruined church at West Hythe, Kent

St Martha's, Surrey

5 Trade Route

The Romans were the great masters of road-building. They made them not for the benefit of the citizens or for trade but so that they might move their armies quickly across the country. Sometimes they found tracks already on the ground which they improved, but for the most part they built new ones.

Certainly many roads already existed, even if they did not match up to Roman standards. Generations of travellers had crossed the

Great-Stone tombs beside the Pilgrims Way.
Above:
Coldrum Stones
Right:
Little Kit's Coty
(The Countless Stones)

country, finding the safest and most convenient routes by trial and error and beating the favoured tracks harder and clearer with their hundreds of feet. These travellers were traders, coming—some of them—from far overseas on their way to such profitable centres of culture as Stonehenge and Avebury and on to the mines of the West Country.

Traders, like invaders, chose, if they could, the shortest sea-route. Many of them arrived on the coast around Dover and made their way westwards along the line of the Downs. Between the windy tops of the hills and the damp and dangerous forests there was a strip where the trees grew thinly and the ground was well drained, and this became their natural way. Gradually a definite track emerged, or more probably two tracks: a higher one for summer, the sheltered lower one for winter use.

When this track was thousands of years old, romantic writers gave it the name of Pilgrims Way, thinking that it had been used by pilgrims travelling between the shrines of St Swithin at Winchester and St Thomas at Canterbury. There is no positive evidence that a single medieval pilgrim ever used the Way, but the name has stuck. You will see on the map—and on the ground if you

Chilham, Kent

Overleaf: The Pilgrims Way passing through Westwell Woods, Kent

Eastern branch of the Pilgrims Way, Stowting, Kent

travel the Way—that it passes to the north of most of the old villages, but, in favour of the 'pilgrim' theory, there are several ancient chapels on the route, like St Catherine's and St Martha's in Surrey, and sacred wells like St Edith's at Kemsing in Kent. Perhaps people believed that a road so ancient and mysterious must be holy.

Along the Way you pass many memorials of pre-Christian Britain, although these are mainly not very conspicuous. Where the track crosses the Medway, however, there are on the hillside the only great-stone tombs surviving in the south-east. Here, where the curving Downs face one another across the tidal river huge stones were piled together to make the chambers of communal graves where the leading families of New Stone Age Kent were buried perhaps four thousand years ago. On the higher slopes, one

Chapel near the Pilgrims Way, West Humble, Surrey

just below, the other just above the Way, are the two best preserved monuments, Coldrum Stones and Kit's Coty. In the valley below are the scattered stones of collapsed tombs at Addington and Little Kit's Coty, while stray stones in the fields and woods—one of them called the White Horse Stone is almost on the Way—may be the remains of other tombs.

At its eastern end the Way has two arms. One, the most familiar, follows the Stour gap to Chilham, where it runs through the middle of that lovely village, and then over sandy hills right through the Iron Age hill-fort of Bigbury; it then becomes a deep rocky track before climbing a last hill and dropping down into Canterbury. The southern arm, less well known and less clear on the ground, crosses the Stour and keeps below the steep slope of the Downs past Folkestone to the coast at Dover. The proposed North Downs Way —a long-distance footpath which is now being planned—will help to reinstate this lost track.

Parties of modern pilgrims sometimes walk the Way from Winchester to Canterbury. Until the North Downs Way is com-

Bridge over Sevenoaks Bypass, Kent

pleted I should not be tempted to do this. For too much of its course the route is now a metalled road; there is not very much motor traffic on it but too much for a walker's comfort. In places, however, it is still a track between hedges or skirting a field or crossing open parkland, and here it rewards the pilgrim richly. Always there are wide views southwards. In Spring the banks are dappled with primroses, wood anemones and white violets. In Autumn you may eat your fill of blackberries.

The best stretches of the Way for walking are, in Surrey, between St Martha's Hill above Guildford and Reigate and, in Kent, between Wrotham and Snodland and, across the Medway, between Hollingbourne and Chilham. At only one point has the Way been deliberately blocked; an eighteenth-century Lord Stanhope decided that he would not tolerate travellers staring at his new house. He enclosed Chevening Park and sent the pilgrims on a long diversion around three sides of a square. Today we have to do the same.

There are many ancient trackways in the south-east. They follow the ridge of the South Downs from east to west, and form the basis of the new South Downs Bridle Way. Other deep rutted tracks cross Down and Weald. Some of these are probably medieval roads linking villages, which have somehow been left out of the modern road system. Many of the Roman roads are hidden under the surface of busy trunk roads, but others you may be able to trace for a mile or two across country; there is a fine course of Stane Street over the South Downs towards Chichester, and near Holtye Common in East Sussex a few yards of the original metalled surface of a military road have been uncovered. All these tracks will give good exercise in historical detection, but the Pilgrims Way offers the longest route and the widest variety of pleasures. Our new motorways are very useful for getting somewhere in a hurry, and when they are well designed they can look very fine in the landscape, but the ancient ways are for those who are more concerned with travelling than with arriving.

6 The Golden Fleece

England's prosperity in the Middle Ages rested on the backs of her sheep. Sheep had been farmed in prehistoric times, but as we have seen the wool industry came into its own after the Black Death. Crop-growing calls for a large number of workmen during most months of the year. A single man with a pair of dogs can manage a flock of sheep, except at lambing and shearing. When half, or a third, of the rural population died of the plague landowners naturally turned to sheep-farming for good practical reasons. The

Sandwich, Kent

Newchurch, one of the great churches of Romney Marsh

wool trade prospered and they enlarged their flocks, even though there were before long sufficient workers for a return to the old-style farming. Soon wool was the principal industry in England, the 'staple' as it was called. Trains of pack animals carrying the raw wool crossed the country, stopping for the night at inns which put up the sign of the Woolpack to attract them. No woolpacks have been seen on the roads for centuries, but Woolpack Inns can be found in all parts of the country where the wool trade flourished.

Men spend their wealth in different ways in different centuries. In the second half of the fourteenth century there was an air of gloom in the land. A huge number of people had died suddenly of a hideous disease. The country was at war, and although there had been brilliant victories at Crecy and Poitiers the enemy had learnt a lesson from disaster and the tide had turned against the English. The peasants had revolted against the miserable life to which they were forced. Old religious ideas were being questioned. Many wealthy people turned from the worries of the present to think about the after-life, and they spent their money in safeguarding their souls.

This was an age of great churches. In the areas of greatest wealth —and that meant the wool areas—little village churches were pulled down and rebuilt in a new and splendid style. They were enlarged by the addition of chantries, small enclosed chapels served by a priest whose job was to pray for the soul of the founder, himself often a woolman.

The south-east seems not to have been as deeply affected as some others were by the craze for rebuilding, or possibly the great cathedral church of Canterbury concentrated attention on its shrines at the expense of lesser places. Although sheep farming was as popular and as profitable here as in places like Yorkshire and East Anglia, there are fewer great parish churches and comparatively more of the older and smaller churches, Norman or even earlier, which escaped rebuilding. It is noticeable, however, that on Romney Marsh, a great centre of sheep-farming, there are several enormous churches in places which could at no time have had enough people to fill them.

At first the wool was mostly exported to the Low Countries and to Germany, where skilled craftsmen turned it into cloth which was then often sold back to English merchants. The biggest profits in the business were lost to the country which produced the raw material. It may have been Edward III's Queen Philippa who first saw the folly of this. She came from Hainault, in the Low Countries, where some of the best cloth-workers lived, and she and the King persuaded some of these craftsmen to settle in England and to carry on their trade here. In the following centuries many other immigrants brought their skills into the country, some of them attracted by the prospect of ample work and wealth, others escaping from tyranny and religious persecution at home.

The immigrants naturally preferred to settle in country which reminded them a little of home. The coastal areas of the south-east were especially favoured, because the low marshy country with its windmills and slow rivers seemed rather like the Netherlands. Industrious and pious foreigners set up house in Canterbury and Sandwich and in the villages and hamlets of Thanet. When, in time, they prospered sufficiently to build their own homes, they often

Flemish gable at Sarre, Kent

Biddenden Cloth Hall, an early industrial building

copied the styles of the old country. In St Peter's-in-Thanet and
Sarre and St Nicholas-at-Wade you will find elegantly curved or
stepped gables in warm Tudor brick which would not look out of
place in Delft or Leyden. Some of these so-called 'Flemish' gables
are imitations of imitations, but some may mark the settlement of
a homesick weaver.

Cloth was originally a cottage industry. The weaver worked in
his own home. In time the trade grew too big for this. Warehouses
were needed for sorting, weighing and storing the cloth. Looms

were too big to fit into an artisan's cottage. A factory was needed, a building large enough to combine workshop, store and master-weaver's house. In the cloth-towns and villages of the Weald, places like Cranbrook and Biddenden, you may find a large house dating from the fifteenth or the sixteenth century with exceptionally high ceilings and tall windows. This is a cloth hall, designed to house the great looms and to give ample light to the workers. These first factories are often extremely handsome buildings.

Trade needs good communications. The wool and cloth merchants of the Middle Ages might make do without good roads, because there was no wheeled traffic and the goods were loaded on pack-saddles. Troubles began when the pack-animals came to a river. A sure-footed horse could ford the stream, but his precious burden might get wet and spoil. The many fine bridges of the south-east, over the Wey in Surrey, the Arun in Sussex, and the Medway and its tributaries in Kent, may be a reminder of the region's wealth in the great age of wool, when the volume of traffic justified the great expense of a stone bridge.

Tilford, Surrey: bridge over the River Wey

Romney Marsh sheep on Pevensey Level, Sussex

Kentish hall-house at Otham. Typical of the homes of prosperous woolmen in the fifteenth and sixteenth centuries

Hammer pond at Witley, Surrey

7 The Iron Age

Ever since the secret of iron was discovered it has been known that there was iron-stone in the Weald. The hope of securing supplies of a valuable war-material was one of the things that encouraged the Romans to undertake the conquest of Britain. Iron-Age settlers braved the perils of the forests to work the iron. A string of hill-forts across the region—Oldbury in Kent, High Rocks and Saxonbury on the Kentish borders of Sussex, Anstiebury, Holm-

63

Hill-top fort at Holmbury, Surrey

Sussex Black Country: the site of Huggett's Furnace

bury and Hascombe along the greensand ridge in Surrey—were probably the refuges made by these primitive miners. The work went on continuously through the centuries, but always on a small scale. The forest was too dense, too difficult to penetrate, still more difficult to get the iron out when it had been found. It was not until almost the close of the Middle Ages that iron-working was taken up in a big commercial way.

Cowden Furnace Pond in Kent and Surrey

THE IRON COUNTRY OF SUSSEX

The two great ponds at Ashburnham were destroyed long ago, but their banks can be seen on either side of a low meadow. The cottage is built on the site of the forge where the iron was hammered out under water-power

Half a mile from Ashburnham is the little village of Penhurst. The manor house, of golden Wealden sandstone, is typical of the fine houses of the prosperous Sussex ironmasters

What doomed the Wealden forest was the invention of gun-powder. This produced a demand for iron far greater than ever before. The ironstone of the Weald was smelted and hammered to make guns, first hand-weapons and land cannon, then bigger guns for the new navy built by King Henry VIII. The demand continued through the sixteenth and seventeenth centuries. In the brief intervals of peace, the iron-masters carried on a profitable trade in ornamental ironwork for the houses of the newly rich, gates guarding the entrance to great houses, firebacks and other hearth furniture, and railings around town houses.

The Weald was well equipped for its share in the industry. It had the raw material. The sandstone beds were rich in iron-ore—and still are, as you will see if you look at an outcrop of rock or a disused quarry or see the rusty stains in the bank of a Wealden stream. It had plenty of fuel. Trees could be cut, stacked, covered and burnt to charcoal, and the supply, it seemed, was endless. The forest was full of little streams, ready to provide water-power when harnessed. Transport was not good, but as the trees were cleared it became steadily easier—although never really easy—to get teams of horses to haul out the worked iron.

For more than two centuries the Weald was the Black Country of England. A watcher on the high ridge of the greensand in those days would have seen a whole constellation of pinpoint lights by night, a forest of smoke-plumes by day, from hundreds of furnaces. Then the industry died. There was no shortage of iron, but in their greed the iron-masters had destroyed the forest and so they ran out of fuel. Coal was discovered in the midlands and the north, and iron began to be worked there. One by one the furnaces went out and the forges fell silent. The iron age was over—Ashburnham Forge in Sussex, the last in the Weald, struggled on until 1828— but it had left its mark on the landscape. The forest had gone. Where once only a few poor peasants ran their half-wild swine, villages, and even little towns like Burwash and Wadhurst, had grown up to provide homes for the workers and the traders who served them. There were roads through the Weald, or at least deep rutted tracks where cannon had been dragged through the sticky mud.

You cannot have industry without power. Power for iron came from water. A stream would be dammed at two points, half a mile or so apart, making two big ponds. At the foot of the first the iron ore was smelted in a charcoal fire. Water racing out of the pond was used to work huge leather bellows to blow the charcoal into great heat. Molten iron was run off and cooled into big oblong 'pigs'. These were taken down to the lower pond, where the water worked a great trip-hammer which beat out the iron in a forge.

Plenty of entertaining detective work can be done while following the footprints of the iron-masters. There are clues everywhere. First, look for place-names. If you find a Forge Farm, see if there is a Furnace Farm a short distance upstream. There may be a house called Chimneys, sometimes Three Chimneys, or a Cinder Farm where the furnace waste was thrown. You may even find the cinders lying undisturbed for three centuries in a woodland thicket.

Next, look for the ponds. When the industry died, some farmers thought that land was more valuable than water and they drained the ponds. Where this happened you must look for unusual depressions in the land on either side of a stream, with an earthen bank running, contrary to nature, across the bottom of the dip. Here and there a pond has survived, where a farmer found a water-supply useful or a wealthy landowner turned it into an ornamental lake. There are fine ponds near Horsham in Sussex, south of Godalming in Surrey, and at Cowden where the boundaries of the three counties meet.

When you are in iron country, look in the village church. Some iron-masters chose to be buried under slabs of iron instead of the traditional stone. You will find slabs, some finely decorated, at Chiddingstone in Kent, Crowhurst in Surrey and Wadhurst in

Sussex. Then look for the homes of the iron-masters. Some of the loveliest houses in the Weald were built out of the profits of iron, including almost the finest of them all. An iron-master built Bateman's, at Burwash in Sussex, in 1634. Nearly three hundred years later Rudyard Kipling came to live here, and in a book he wrote in the house—*Puck of Pook's Hill*—he painted a picture of Sussex in the Age of Iron.

The Norman keep at Guildford, Surrey

8 Conqueror's Castles

On 28th September 1066, Duke William of Normandy landed with an invasion force on the shores of Sussex below the ruined walls of a Roman coastal fort at Pevensey. It was a curious place to choose, because beyond the fort there were miles of difficult and dangerous marsh in which an army could be bogged down or lost. Perhaps the landing was accidental, for the Normans, in spite of their Norse origin, were indifferent navigators. From Pevensey the invaders made their way to Hastings, where they threw up hurried fortifications, and they then marched inland to meet the English army on

Dover Castle

Dover Castle keep

the slopes of a low Wealden hill. The place, nameless then, has ever since been called Battle.

After the Battle of Hastings and the formal submission of the English, William the Conqueror found himself with two countries to rule. Both were likely to prove difficult and had to be held by force. William controlled his new kingdom, as he did his old dukedom, through a network of castles.

One of his first concerns was to secure the routes between London and Normandy. The key was the old Roman road to the port of Dover, and this had to be guarded at two principal river-crossings at Rochester and Canterbury. Another and more difficult track led from London to Hastings, with a crossing of the Medway at Tonbridge. Then the chief ports of the Channel coast needed to be guarded. This done, the Conqueror could hope to move freely between his two realms.

The captains of William's force were old and trusted friends, and to them he gave the key fortresses along the Channel. William de Warenne, a close friend and possibly the Conqueror's son-in-law, held Lewes, on a hill commanding the gap of the River Ouse through the South Downs, and William de Braose had a rather similar position for his castle on the Adur at Bramber. With such men in charge the King might expect these strongholds to remain faithful to him—but not, as it proved, necessarily faithful to his sons.

A few castles were built in stone from the start. Most of them, for speed and cheapness, were of earth. These motte-and-bailey castles consisted of a steep, flat-topped mound about 50 feet high

The barbican of Lewes Castle, Sussex

The ruined shell of the keep, Rochester Castle, Kent

—the motte standing within a raised flat platform called a bailey. Both were surrounded by deep ditches filled with water. There was a high wooden fence around the bailey and another defended the flat top of the motte. In the south-east many of these castles were later remodelled in stone, but a few remain in their original form, notably a fine motte at Abinger in Surrey.

Even where a surviving castle is now of stone, it is possible to see how it grew out of a motte-and-bailey. Arundel Castle—one of the few which are still the homes of their owners—has changed greatly since it was first built to hold the Arun gap through the Downs, but its original plan is still clear. A round tower—called a shell keep—sits around the motte which has on either side a bailey lined with buildings. These double baileys were not uncommon. Lewes, however, shows the rare example of a double motte; one now has a stone keep on top, while the other stands overgrown and neglected across the central bailey.

The rigid discipline of the first Norman kings broke down after the death of Henry I, and in Stephen's reign each baron became his own master and built a castle to protect himself from his enemies and to provide a base from which he could ravage the surrounding country. Henry II destroyed many of these unofficial fortresses when he established a strong central rule again. During his reign most of the licensed castles—his own and those of reliable followers—were rebuilt in stone. This was the age of the tall square keep, modelled on the earlier example of the Tower of London. Rochester keep, which was of this style, had been built earlier, during Stephen's troubles, but the great keep of Dover dates from Henry II's reign and so do the keeps of Guildford in Surrey and Chilham in Kent. At the same time a tall wall was built around the bailey with towers at each angle; this remains almost perfect at Dover.

A few castles in the south-east lost their importance early in the Middle Ages. Guildford, built to control the crossing of the Wey at a gap in the North Downs, and Reigate, a fortress of the Warennes of Lewes, seem to have had fairly short histories as strategic castles. Others continued to be useful and were adapted to conform with changing ideas about military architecture. The round tower was evolved to resist undermining and blows from siege engines. Crusaders brought back the idea of the 'concentric' castle, with two walled baileys, one inside the other. The keep went out of fashion, and a great gatehouse became the principal fortification. There is a fine gatehouse, from Edward I's reign, grafted on to the motte-and-bailey castle of the Clare family at Tonbridge, and the Constable's Gate which guards the main entrance at Dover is of the same date.

Many of the castles of the south-east are now in ruins. This is not often just the result of great age. The Norman castle at Eynsford in Kent was abandoned in the twelfth century, and no building will survive such long neglect. Some were deliberately ruined during

Arundel, Sussex

the Civil War of the seventeenth century to prevent their use against the Government. A few are still lived in. Leeds, a small royal castle in Kent which by long tradition was granted to the queen, had a mock 'castle' added to it early in the nineteenth century and it still makes a pleasant moated home. Arundel looks almost too picturesque to be true, and certainly many of its elegant buildings were added or lavishly restored by the Howards who owned it, but it is an appropriately splendid home for the Earl Marshal of England.

The most convincing castle which survives in the south-east is Dover, which housed a military garrison from William the Conqueror until after the Second World War. Much of its architectural detail has been changed because of the need to keep it always in a state of readiness for action, but this, rather than spoiling it, makes it the more exciting. Here is the key to the gate of England, which shows, not artificially for the amusement of tourists but realistically, every change in methods of defence over nine hundred years. And, if you include the Roman lighthouse which stands at the highest point, another seven hundred are added to the story.

Waverley Abbey, Surrey

9 God's Work and Man's

The duty of a monk was to pray to God. This he did almost literally day and night, for his 'day' started at 2.30 in the morning. Between services he had to fit in as best he could all the other jobs required of him.

In spite of this the abbeys performed many very important functions. They were, some of them, great centres of learning. Abbot Hadrian came from Africa, by way of Rome, to make St Augustine's Abbey in Canterbury a place to which scholars came from all over Christendom. St Augustine's and the neighbouring

St Augustine's Abbey, Canterbury

*Looking westward across the ruins of St Augustine's Abbey
to Canterbury Cathedral*

Priory of Christ Church (the Cathedral) were rivals for centuries
in their schools and their libraries, and Durham Cathedral-Priory
was almost as famous in the north. Some abbeys became well-
known as centres of painting and penmanship, and the manuscript
books made in them were treasured by kings and bishops. Every
abbey offered hospitality to those on the road. The abbot or the
prior welcomed royal and noble travellers, and the almoner gave
humbler fare to the wayfaring poor. Lastly the monasteries accepted
responsibility for charitable work, feeding the hungry and healing
—as far as they could—the sick.

The monks, in fact, had to work *and* pray. The proportion of
prayer to work depended upon the Order to which they belonged.
The first abbey to be founded in England, apart from the Celtic
monasteries of the north and west, was the Abbey of St Peter and
St Paul which Augustine established in Canterbury immediately

*Waverley Abbey,
Surrey: the first house
of Cistercians monks in
England*

*Wilmington Priory,
Sussex: a manor of the
abbey of Grestain in
Normandy*

after his conversion of the King of Kent, and which was later given the founder's name. St Augustine's was a Benedictine house; that is, it followed the rules laid down by St Benedict which made prayer the monk's first duty, followed by work. Later a new Order appeared called Cluniac, after the Abbey of Cluny in France. This insisted on a very elaborate and beautiful form of service. By the end of the eleventh century the Benedictines had lost their early enthusiasm, and a reformed Order was founded at the Abbey of Citeaux. These monks were called Cistercians. They believed that it was not good to live, as the Benedictines did, in cities and towns. The Cistercians built their abbeys in remote country places. In England their first house was Waverley Abbey in Surrey, in a lonely valley beside the River Wey. They preferred a very plain life and their buildings were bare and without ornament. On their deserted sites they worked hard to cultivate the land, and their energy and efficient management in turn made them very rich. The abbots, originally so saintly, became businessmen and politicians.

A stream of the Kentish Stour flowing through Greyfriars, Canterbury

Capital in the Norman chapel of St Nicholas, Harbledown, Kent

As time went on the successful monasteries became bigger, with enormous churches and an elaborate collection of buildings to house the monks and their servants. Others failed to find rich patrons or holy relics to attract pilgrims and so remained quite small. Large and small, however, they attracted the attention of Henry VIII in his search for power and wealth, and they were all closed and the monks—at least those who accepted their fate without argument—pensioned off.

The finest remains of medieval abbeys are in the north and west, where the buildings were protected by their remoteness. In the busy south-east most of the buildings were quickly destroyed, unless, like Christ Church in Canterbury, they still served a useful purpose as the cathedral, or, like Battle Abbey, a new owner built his house inside the abbey. The only monastic ruin in the region to be compared with the great abbeys of Yorkshire is at Bayham in

Abbot's Hospital, Guildford, Surrey

Sussex, a Premonstratensian abbey—the Premonstratensians were canons, that is priests, who followed an Order rather like that of the Cistercians—on a site which, because it is on a private estate, has remained almost as quiet as when it was founded.

The closing of the monasteries destroyed a very important source of charity. Not all the abbeys had done this work well, but it was better than nothing, and with the abbeys gone nothing remained. It was an age of great poverty and suffering. A few hospitals survived, like St Nicholas at Harbledown, which the Norman Archbishop Lanfranc had founded as a home for lepers. Most of the newly rich gentry were too concerned with increasing their wealth to bother about the poor, but one or two showed that they had a conscience. At Cobham, in Kent, a college of priests had been suppressed and left to fall into ruin. Lord Cobham restored the buildings, added to them and turned the college into an almshouse where poor old people of the neighbourhood might end their days.

Lord Cobham was able to use an existing building. When the Archbishop of Canterbury, George Abbot, decided to found a hospital in his home town, Guildford, he put it on a fine new site at the top of the steep High Street and built it with gatehouse, quadrangle, Master's lodge, hall and chapel like an Oxford college. Abbot's Hospital was built in 1617. In the same year Sackville College was founded at East Grinstead in Sussex. This is a very handsome building, on the same lines as Abbot's but more elaborate. It is built of local sandstone and has, as well as the usual hall and chapel for the inmates, a separate range with hall and kitchen at the rear. This was for the use of the founder, the Earl of Dorset—one of the Sackvilles of Withyham and Knole—when he was travelling in these parts.

Abbot and Sackville had, no doubt, a genuine wish to help the poor, but they knew, too, that these grand buildings would keep their memory alive. Humbler people remembered the needs of their neighbours in a more modest way. If you go into a village church you may find, on the wall at the rear or in the ground floor of the tower, a wooden board painted with elegant lettering of the eighteenth century which records local charities. Here are the names of men and women who gave money and land for the benefit of poor parishioners. Some of these charities are still active, providing food for old-age pensioners at Christmas or a scholarship at a public school.

Sackville College, Sussex

10 Rude Forefathers

When the great lord wanted a new house, or the bishop a new cathedral, he would send for expert craftsmen to look for the best materials, not hesitating to send halfway across the kingdom or overseas for the right quality of stone. The farmer, the parish priest and the cottager made do with what was nearest to hand, both in materials and in workmen. We have come to value the humble village cottage, churches, barns and mills, finding them as attractive and as valuable in their ways as the great palaces of the rich.

Cranbrook Mill, Kent

Flint cottage at Goodwood, Sussex

The heading for this chapter comes from a poem in which Thomas Gray, a scholarly writer of the eighteenth century, thinks about all the ordinary people whose lives have gone quietly towards the making of history. It reminds me of another poet, this time from the south-east—Edmund Blunden—who grew up in a Kentish village and who learnt to love the men whom he saw at work and play. They were not 'clever' people but they were masters of their own jobs. As Blunden says in *Forefathers*:

> . . . *Scarce could read or hold a quill,*
> *Built the barn, the forge, the mill.*

If you look around you in Blunden's countryside you will find great barns, and forges—or the remains of them—and water- and wind-mills, which will show how well our forefathers built.

Our forefathers used local materials for building. Going about the south-east, examining cottages and farm buildings—and ignoring those which are less than two hundred years old—you will get a clear idea of how rural craftsmen used brick and stone and timber, and how the materials and the tools guided them to build in particular styles. Countrymen were not much affected by changes in fashion, and so they built as their great-grandfathers had done. We think of a black-and-white timbered building as 'Tudor' and so it may be. It may just as likely be two centuries later than Queen Elizabeth's reign, put up by a man who used without thinking materials and tools and ideas which were second-nature to him.

The south-east is not rich in local stone. In the Weald there is a rusty-gold sandstone which works well, although it may wear badly, and in this central belt plenty of farmhouses and cottages use this material. The greensand ridge around Maidstone produces Kentish rag, a hard grey stone. Ragstone gives a rough effect which is pleasing in church towers and garden walls. In houses it looks

Surrey tile-hanging and brick at Dunsfold

Thatch, near Yalding,
Kent

Weatherboard cottage
at Egerton, Kent

rather gloomy. The building-stone of the Downs is flint. Anyone who has seen a downland field after ploughing knows that there is plenty of flint about. It is a very tough material which can be used whole—showing the thin white 'skin' around the nodule—or split to show a beautiful shiny blue surface. It is not easy to handle well, but many downland cottages, barns, walls and towers show evidence of the skill of the old craftsmen.

The forest areas had abundant supplies of wood, and buildings in timber are plentiful. Timber-framed ('half-timber') houses were originally filled in with plaited wattle smeared with clay to keep out the wind. Nowadays this is usually replaced with brick. Sometimes

Oast kilns at Chart Sutton, Kent

Right: Windmills on South Downs, above Clayton, Sussex

Below: Haxted watermill, Surrey

the timber frame is covered with overlapping weatherboard, or the upper half of the house may be covered with tiles skilfully hung on wooden pegs. Mostly the work is plain, avoiding the extravagant ornamental black-and-white which you find in the north-midlands. At most a porch may be supported by a pair of grotesque monsters, or some of the tiles may be shaped like fishes' tails.

There are some fine flint barns in the Downs, but most of those in the south-east are timber-framed with a covering of weatherboard. Originally windmills were usually made of wood. It was not uncommon for them to be moved from one site to another, and it must have looked strange as the huge ungainly structure was carried along on a waggon. Once in position on a breezy height there is nothing clumsy about a mill. It is perhaps the most beautiful machine which man has invented. The windmill is entirely functional; there is not a wasted inch anywhere. The lines are clean and there is no fussy detail; everything is there for use. Watermills look quite different but they work on the same principle, using water-power to turn the great gears as the windmill uses air. The south-eastern windmills ground corn or drained marshland. The watermills might be used for corn, or for making paper, or for fulling—putting 'body' into loosely woven cloth. Many have been demolished but you may be able to trace them, windmills by place-names or by the mill-base, a flattened circular mound which looks rather like a squat Norman motte, watermills by place-names or by the surviving millponds and races which show how, even on the smallest streams, the miller borrowed power, used it, and then passed it on to his neighbour downstream.

The most familiar and attractive of workaday buildings in the south-east is the oast. Hops have been grown here since Tudor times, mainly in Kent and east Sussex but also in parts of Surrey, but it is now an important crop only in Kent. When the hop is ripe it is picked and dried before being packed into a tall sack—called a pocket—for storage. The tall round or square kiln called an oast was designed as a drying chamber some time in the first

Aylesford, Kent: Norman church, fifteenth-century bridge, ancient and modern cottages, all living together in harmony

quarter of the nineteenth century. The tapering roof makes a funnel to provide the right draught and the white cone on top rotates to match changes in the direction of the wind. It was—and still is —a matter of pride for the farmer to put his sign on the vane which sticks out to catch the wind, usually the rampant white horse which is the Kentish badge, sometimes a more stolid cart horse on all fours; you may find variants, crows or pheasants instead of horses, with farm-names to match.

When better roads and transport made it possible to move building materials cheaply the old local crafts died. Today there is little to distinguish a new Sussex house from one in Lancashire or Devon; both are likely to be made of brick or concrete, and they may both follow the same developer's plan. For this reason, you may find that the new building sits less comfortably in the landscape than the old. A village street will have houses of all ages between the fifteenth and the eighteenth centuries. They probably all look different and yet each gets on well, visually, with its neighbours. Most of the new houses are not good neighbours, and it is not merely because they look new. We can build individual fine houses today, but somehow we seem to have lost the art of blending houses. Where a new village or estate has been planted, it lacks the harmony which we find in villages like Slindon in Sussex, or Shere in Surrey, or Aylesford in Kent, where generations of rural craftsmen, without deliberately planning to do so, have set old and new, grand and homely, in a satisfying whole.

Clandon Park, Surrey

11 Family Trees

The great families of medieval Kent, Sussex and Surrey—the Warennes, the Montgomeries and the Clares—have all gone. Their houses are vanished, or in ruins, and their names remembered only in the history books. (You may, however, see the tomb of William de Warenne and his wife Gundrada in Southover Church. They were buried in the priory of St Pancras which they had founded at Lewes. At the Reformation the tomb was destroyed, its fine carved top taken to the little church of Isfield higher up the River Ouse, and the memory of the founders forgotten. Then, when the railway

99

Nettlestead, Kent

Penshurst Place, Kent: home of the Sidneys for more than four hundred years

was built through Lewes workmen dug through the site of the high altar of the priory church and hit upon the coffins of William and his wife. A little chapel was built for them in the nearby church and the original tomb slab was brought back and laid over them.)

After the turmoil of the French wars, the civil Wars of the Roses, and the executions by which the Tudors protected their throne, few of the old families were left. Their place was taken by a new aristocracy, wealthy traders and politicians, who built themselves stately houses. Many of these houses remain, some of them still occupied by descendants of the original owners. Mores of Loseley, Sackvilles of Knole, Wyndhams—descended on the female side from the Tudor Percys—of Petworth, these families continue in their old settings, even if their houses may sometimes belong to the National Trust and they live in them as tenants. We may have the privilege of visiting these great houses, to see the fine architecture and decoration and the works of art with which they are filled, and to notice how much more homelike the largest house is when it is lived in by people who love it and share its history.

Many of the great houses have admitted visitors for centuries, like Penshurst Place in Kent. The personal name of Viscount de L'Isle, who lives there now, is Philip Sidney. His ancestor, another Philip Sidney, was born in the ancient manor house in 1554. When he was a young man his father decided to enlarge the family home, and he gave his son the job of supervising the rebuilding. The great Renaissance palace which we visit today, and which encloses the original house like a skin, grew up under Philip Sidney's eye. Then he left Penshurst to go to Queen Elizabeth's Court, winning fame as a poet and a scholar; from there he went to fight in his uncle Leicester's army in the Netherlands where he died, making one of those grand gestures, sincere yet dramatic, which seemed to come so easily to the Elizabethans.

Not all the great houses of the south-east have remained homes. The Knatchbulls have left Mersham-le-Hatch—although they have not gone far away—and the magnificent house designed by

Gatton, Surrey: the family has gone and the great house is now a school

Knole, Kent: the Sackvilles came to Knole in the reign of Queen Elizabeth I

*Their previous home was at Buckhurst, Sussex, and the family continued
to be buried in the parish church at Withyham, Sussex*

*Above: Robert Adams build Mersham-le-Hatch for the Kentish Knatch-
bulls about 1766. Below: Later members of the family preferred to be
buried at Smeeth, and their arms are displayed there*

In crucifixa gloria mea.

Robert Adam is now used for fine work with deprived children. Gatton, which stands in a superb setting on the North Downs, is a school. In its great day the estate—there was no village—was a borough returning two members to Parliament and the owner of the Hall was sometimes the only voter. Wootton Place in Surrey, the old home of the Evelyns, one of whom was the John Evelyn who kept a diary in which he described the Great Plague and the Great Fire of London, is now, perhaps appropriately, a training college for the Fire Service.

Men like Sir Philip Sidney and the first Sackville of Knole were important figures in national history. Others made no impression on the nation but still played a notable part in local affairs. One cannot follow the story of the south-east without knowing something about them. But when the family is gone, often the house too, where can one find clues to the lives of these vanished worthies?

The village church will probably show some evidence. The great families were much concerned with leaving the right kind of memory behind them, and every nobleman and most gentlemen left precise instructions about where and in what style they were to be buried. Often they preferred to lie in the parish church of their old home. The Sackvilles made Knole their principal residence from the first years of the seventeenth century, but they were buried not at Sevenoaks but at Withyham, near their original Sussex house of Buckhurst. If you visit this little church you will find that they employed the best sculptors of the day to carve their monuments.

The inscriptions on tombs, in good plain Latin in early times, get longer and more elaborate with the passing centuries. To read them you would think that every worthy was a saint. The epitaphs may tell white lies, but the sculptor was often honest and the marble portraits of fat-jowled, arrogant nobles tell you a great deal about them.

Most memorials include a display of the family arms. Heraldry often offers accurate clues to the past, because the arms survive even after every memory of the family has vanished. You will find heraldic evidence in stained glass. The window illustrated on page 98 was designed when the village church at Nettlestead was rebuilt at the expense of the family from the stone-built Place next door. Reginald de Pympe put into the design his own arms and those of his relatives, as well as the arms of those who had fought with him at Agincourt.

One curious custom of the eighteenth century has produced useful evidence. When a local notable died, his arms, painted on a board of canvas and wood, was hung outside the mourning house;

Funeral hatchment at Slaugham, Sussex

Lewes, Sussex

then after the funeral it was placed in the church. When the original had been forgotten these hatchments were often thrown away but many still remain. Dusty and fading, they still display arms which show the union of once-famous families as well as the motto RESURGAM which proclaims the worthy's hope of resurrection.

A wealthy nobleman who owned property in many parts of the country was the patron, or owner, of inns and these displayed his arms on their signboards. You will see the Abergavenny Arms at Frant, near the gates of Eridge Castle. The Nevills, Earls of Abergavenny, still live there and their badge, a bull's head, can be seen on cottages on the estate. They no longer have a seat at Birling, in Kent, but the village inn is called the Nevill Bull. My picture on page 106 shows the Pelham Arms in Lewes. The Pelhams were one of the greatest of Sussex families, and at one time there were probably many of these signs above wayside inns. The curious device, rather like a stirrup, on either side of the shield is the Pelham Buckle. Sir John Pelham was with the Black Prince at the Battle of Poitiers and captured the French King John. So did several other knights and there was a great squabble over the royal prisoner. The Prince took charge of King John and he rewarded Pelham with the buckle from his belt, which he and his descendants took as their badge. It crops up throughout east Sussex wherever this very wealthy family owned property, to remind us of the blood and dust of a September day of 1356 below the walls of Poitiers.

(I should add that historians no longer believe this story, putting it into the same class as Alfred's cakes among historical tales which are too good to be true.)

Hales Place, Tenterden, Kent

12 Living in a Picture

The medieval lord made a home of his castle, but it was so important to keep out uninvited guests that home comfort came a very long way after security. It took centuries for people to come round to thinking that pleasant surroundings mattered to them. A few Crusaders saw that the Saracens enjoyed a finer style of living than they did, but fewer still tried to copy their enemies when they got home. It was not until the end of the Middle Ages that a new wealthy class of merchants turned their backs on the warlike pastimes of the rich and set about enjoying their leisure.

Triumphal arch at Mereworth Castle, Kent

Cobham Hall, Kent: garden house

'Witch's Cottage' at Knole, Kent

The Tudor age was the first great age of gardening. Very formal gardens were laid out beside the tall brick mansions, often within high brick walls which trapped the sun. Changing fashions in gardening in later centuries have destroyed the Tudor gardens, but here and there the bare bones of them—the walls and terraces —remain. There are two gardens in Kent—Hales Place in Tenterden and Roydon Hall at East Peckham—which have high walls of dark red Tudor brick and battlemented turrets at the corners. A century earlier the turrets would have been for defence; now the builder is mocking his past fears and making fortifications for fun.

In the following century the passion for gardening grew. Noblemen who went into exile with the King during the Civil War were

LANDSCAPES WITH TREES
*Above: Sheffield Park, Sussex: an eighteenth-century design setting off the
mock-Gothic mansion. Below: Wierton, Kent: an ornamental avenue now
bordering farmland*

attracted to the fine new houses in France and Holland with their grand avenues and fountains. When they came home again they imitated these splendid gardens in their own estates. Gardens of this kind, like the Tudor gardens, were obviously artificial. There was no attempt to imitate nature; instead the gardener, working with living trees and flowers, and also statues and stone ornaments, made a work of art.

This kind of garden lasted well into the eighteenth century until it was replaced by another fashion, the copying of nature. Builders of very formal grand houses in the classical Italian style surrounded them, rather oddly, with landscapes which set out to improve on nature. The rise and fall of the land was altered to provide a more interesting scene, trees and evergreen shrubs were planted in carefully chosen positions, and 'eye-catchers', little garden houses

Modern landscape design, Wisley, Surrey

*The Mote, Maidstone, Kent: Lord Romney looked across the artificial
lake to the classical temple put up in his honour in 1801*

shaped like Greek temples, classical statues, imitation ruined abbeys and castles—were built on sites to which the viewer's eye was led up open vistas between the wooded groves.

There were stages in the development of this landscape gardening, associated with the names of the artists who introduced them, men like William Kent, Lancelot ('Capability') Brown and Humphry Repton. Their techniques were different, but they all had the same idea, to make pictures for the wealthy to live in.

The first essential of a landscape garden was a ha-ha. The immediate surroundings of the house had to merge into the park with no apparent boundary, so that the owner looking through his window would see only fine avenues and clumps. Cattle, sheep and deer grazed the park, however, and these must not be allowed near the house. Instead of a fence, which would spoil the illusion of open country, the landscape gardener built a ha-ha, a deep ditch, cut sharply on the inner side and lined with stone or brick. The outer bank sloped down gently to the bottom of the ditch. This made an effective but—from a distance—invisible barrier. There are ha-has in good order at Chilham Castle and Penshurst, both in Kent, and in many other places.

Landscape gardening, although it was on such a huge scale, depended on fine detail. There must be no false notes in the scene. A homely building like a keeper's cottage still had to look just right in its setting. At Knole the Sackvilles made one like a witch's cottage, turning the chimney stacks into tall conical hats, and then they built the broken walls of a sham ruined abbey around it.

Water was an important material of landscape gardening. If a stream ran through the estate it would be dammed to make a lake, ornamental but, because it followed the line of the valley, seemingly natural. A great lake is the centrepiece of Capability Brown's design at Petworth, in Sussex, and in the same county he created a chain of lakes at Sheffield Park. At Painshill in Surrey the River Mole flowed away from the estate, so the designer pumped water from it to fill his lakes. No engineering enterprise was too difficult in making these formal stretches of water.

Trees mature slowly, and the creators of landscape gardens never saw them fully grown, except in their imagination. Today most of them are a little past their best, but still very beautiful. Brown's garden at Sheffield has been changed and enriched by planting a wider range of trees around his lakes, notably colourful maples, and the Victorian passion for flowering shrubs intruded alien tones into many Georgian scenes. Enough remains to show what remarkable artists these eighteenth century masters were, who painted their masterpieces in grass and water and foliage.

Many of the great landowners have gone and their estates have

Herstmonceux Observatory

been broken up. The demand for land, especially in time of war when food must be grown at home, has meant that old parkland has been ploughed for corn. The ground-plan of the landscape garden sometimes survives. An avenue of elms along the side of a field, or a geometrically round clump of trees on the crown of a hill, may be all that remains of a design worked out by Brown or Repton two hundred years ago.

Even the richest landowners now plan their gardens on a smaller scale than this. The big landscape gardens of today are the botanical gardens at Kew and Wakehurst and the Royal Horticultural Society's plots at Wisley. Something of Brown's influence remains, for these estates made for scientific experiments are also very beautiful. The scientist too lives in a picture.

Index